The
PROFESSIONAL
FLORAL DESIGN
Manual

afs

This manual is dedicated to
Eulalah Overmeyer, AAF, AIFD, PFCI,
AFS Vice President of Education, Emeritus.
Known as "The First Lady of Floriculture",
her commitment to education inspires
all of us to believe in ourselves, our talents and
our ability to make a difference.

Preface

Why a book on professional floral design? Students of the AFS Education Center have asked if there was one source—a book—that could clearly and simply explain the principles and elements of floral design. We found it tough to recommend just one source. Until now.

The staff of PFD carefully researched rules and vocabulary from design fields closest to floral design: art, architecture, photography, music and jewelry design. The members of the AFS Creative Team added to this project by creating beautiful design examples to illustrate each subject.

Each section of the book builds the foundation for the next section. We begin with the principles: Composition, Unity, Proportion, Accent, Balance, Harmony and Rhythm. Then, we discuss the elements: Line, Form, Space, Texture and Color. Finally, we focus on design Forms, Techniques and Styles.

As an added value, we've included a glossary to provide you with precise definitions of the terms we've used to explain the rules. We've also included an informative section on the care and handling of flowers. To give you a handy way of checking the spelling of flowers you use in your shop, we've added an alphabetical list of common name spellings of flowers, foliages and plants.

The result of all this information being gathered is a book the AFS Education Center is proud to recommend. It's about time that beginners had a single source to turn to for insight into the rules of floral design. Seasoned designers will also find this book a great reference tool for teaching and sharing design theory with students and audiences.

We hope that you develop a clearer understanding of the fundamentals through this book, and continually strive to improve your own design skills.

Jim Morley, AAF, AIFD, PFCI
Editor

THE PROFESSIONAL FLORAL DESIGN MANUAL

Editor: Jim Morley, AAF, AIFD, PFCI
Associate Editor: Marie Ackerman, AIFD, PFCI

DESIGN STAFF
Lisa Albrecht, AIFD
Allen Beck, AIFD
Frank Brice, AIFD
Haskell Eargle, AIFD
Mark Erickson, AIFD
Hitomi Gilliam, AIFD
John Haines, AIFD
Els Hazenberg, AIFD
Tom Powell, AIFD
David Siders, AIFD
Bill Taylor, AIFD
Bob Wietholter

Product Coordinator: Donna Morley
Photography: Sanford Mauldin Photographer,
        Norman, OK
        deGennaro Associates,
        Los Angeles, CA

The Professional Floral Design Manual was designed,
written, edited, produced and published by The AFS
Education Center. American Floral Services, Inc.,
P.O. Box 12309, Oklahoma City, OK 73157-2309.

First edition published in December 1989 by American
Floral Services, Inc. in the United States of America.

Second printing in September 1990.

Third printing in March 1993.

Fourth printing in July 1994.

Fifth printing in April 1995.

Sixth printing in April 1997.

Seventh printing in November 1998.

Library of Congress Catalog No. 89-81580
ISBN 0-944074-01-4

Printed and bound in Oklahoma City, OK, USA.
$24.95 U.S. Funds

ABOUT THE AFS EDUCATION CENTER

Established in 1983 by American Floral Services, Inc., the
AFS Education Center teaches and trains thousands of retail
florists each year. The center is located in the American
Floral Services Home Office in Oklahoma City, Oklahoma.
The training facility provides education in floral design,
commentating, management and computer operation.
Equipped with workroom, lecture room and computer class-
room the center has state-of-the-art sound systems, flower
shop equipment, audio-visual and multi-media capabilities,
and personal computers. Each year the AFS Education
Center offers a series of seminars in advanced floral design,
computer use, management and commentating. The instructors
are from all over North America and Europe and are highly
qualified and proven successful in their subject matter. In
addition to the seminars at the center in Oklahoma City, the
AFS Education Center presents educational programs
throughout the United States, Canada and foreign countries.
The AFS Education Center also publishes PFD, a floral design
magazine, six times a year and has published several books
for point-of-purchase use and as educational tools for the
retail florist.

TABLE OF CONTENTS

QUICK REFERENCE GLOSSARY 4, 5

DESIGN PRINCIPLES 6-13
  Composition 6
  Unity 7, 8
  Proportion 9
  Accent 10
  Balance 11
  Harmony 12
  Rhythm 13

DESIGN ELEMENTS 14-24
  Line 14, 15
  Form 16
  Space 17, 18
  Texture 19
  Color 20-24
    Monochromatic 20
    Analogous 21
    Complementary 22
    Split Complement 23
    Triadic 24

DESIGN FORMS 25-33
  Symmetrical Triangle 25
  Asymmetrical Triangle 26
  Horizontal 27
  Vertical 28
  Circular 29
  Oval 30
  Fan-Shape 31
  Crescent 32
  Hogarth Curve 33

DESIGN TECHNIQUES 34-47
  Basing 34
  Focal Area 35
  Terracing 36, 37
  Grouping 38
  Clustering 39
  Zoning 40
  Sequencing 41
  Banding 42
  Binding 43
  Shadowing 44, 45
  Framing 46
  Parallelism 47

TRADITIONAL DESIGN STYLES 48-52
  Biedermeier 48
  Mille de Fleur 49
  Waterfall 50, 51
  Phoenix 52

NATURAL DESIGN STYLES 53-56
  Botanical 53
  Radial Vegetative 54
  Parallel Vegetative 55
  Landscape 56

LINEAR DESIGN STYLES 57-60
  Western Line 57
  Parallel Systems 58
  New Convention 59
  Formal Linear 60

EXPERIMENTAL DESIGN STYLES 61-64
  Pavé 61
  Pillowing 62
  New Wave 63
  Abstract 64

COMMON NAME SPELLING GUIDE FOR FLOWERS,
  FOLIAGES AND PLANTS 65

THE PROPER CARE AND HANDLING OF
  FRESH FLOWERS 66, 67

TIPS ON THE CARE AND HANDLING
  OF FLOWERS 68, 69

INDEX 70

QUICK REFERENCE GLOSSARY

A

Abstract —|style| Free form designs focusing on unconventional or radical mechanical techniques. Emphasis on color, shape or texture.

Accent —|design principle| A distinctive regularly occurring but, subordinate motif, pattern or color.

Analogous Color Harmony — One primary hue plus adjacent colors on the color wheel forming a 90 degree angle.

Asymmetrical Balance —|one type of balance| Unequal visual weight on either side of an axis.

Asymmetrical Triangle —|design form| A triangle with unequal visual weight on either side of its center axis. Two types: right triangle and scalene triangle.

B

Balance —|design principle| The placement of ingredients to create physical and visual stability. Three types are possible: symmetrical, asymmetrical and open.

Banding —|technique| A thin, flat strip of material surrounding a stem or container for decorative purposes.

Basing —|technique| Materials in a design's foundation which give the design and the materials emerging from it visual stability.

Biedermeier —|style| Influenced by a period in German and Austrian history|1815-1848| this style of design features compact circular and oval forms and concentric material placement.

Binding —|technique| The process of uniting three or more like materials by tying them together in bunches.

Binding Point —|also known as bindary point| The imaginary point where all stems of a design would intersect, if extended.

Botanical —|style| A design representing a study in the structure, properties and processes of plant life. Life cycle of roots, leaves, flowers and the end of a flower's life are depicted.

C

Chroma —|color theory| The degree of intensity or purity of a hue, used to express the difference between a bright color and a duller shade.

Circular Form — Sphere-like appearance. All materials radiate from a single point within the container.

Classic Form — A timeless design shape that expresses simple harmony.

Closed Form — A term used to describe a massed, compact or solid area design perimeter.

Clustering —|technique| A collection of like materials placed so closely together in a design that quantity, shape or number cannot be determined. Materials lose identity and function as one unit.

Complementary Color Harmony — Two hues that lie directly opposite from each other on the color wheel.

Composition —|design principle| An organization or grouping of different parts to achieve a unified whole.

Crescent Form — The three dimensional portion of a circle |like the moon in its first quarter| created by the organization of floral materials.

D

Design — A planned organization of materials for a specific purpose.

Dynamic Line —|one type of line| An active line of continuous movement that counters a design's form. Example: A curving line within a rectangular format is considered dynamic.

E

Elements of Design —|line, form, space, texture and color| The interpretive components used at the discretion of the designer to create distinctive floral designs.

Equilateral Triangle —|form| All sides of a triangle are equal in length.

Extended Analogous Color Harmony — Analogous colors |one pure hue plus adjacent colors forming a 90° angle| plus the color |or colors| on either side of the 90° section.

F

Fan-shape —|form| A radial style, half circle design.

Focal Area — A large area |with more than one ingredient| emphasized by the contrast of materials. The place or places within a design which capture the eye of the viewer.

Focal Point — A single point in a design from which all materials meet and radiate.

Form —|design element| The three dimensional external appearance of an area distinguished by the materials of a composition.

Formal Linear —|style| Clearly defined lines and angles with asymmetrical balance. Design focuses on shape and form of materials and how they fit together.

Framing —|technique| Materials in the perimeter of a design fully or partially enclosing an area and focusing attention to its contents.

G

Grouping —|technique| Identical materials in a design placed in a specific, limited area with space between the individual parts.

H

Harmony —|design principle| The pleasing aesthetic quality created by the careful placement of materials within a composition. Harmony can be expressed with similar or dissimilar materials.

Hogarth Curve —|form| An s-shape form made from floral materials. Interpreted from the "Line of Beauty" pioneered by English Painter William Hogarth |1697-1764|.

Horizontal —|form| A low, flat and tranquil horizontal flow of materials. When extended the length is 1 1/2 to 2 times the length of the focal area.

Hue —|color theory| The name of a full intensity color. The name could be simple, like red, or compounded like blue-violet.

I

Intermediate Colors —|also known as tertiary colors| Colors created by combining a primary color with a secondary color. Example: Intermediate red-orange is created by mixing primary red and secondary orange.

Interpretive Design — A variation of a style, technique or combination of ingredients that deviates from true-form specifications.

Isosceles Triangle — |form| A triangle with two sides equal in length, one side is different.

L

Landscape — |style| A design resembling a large dimensional view of a garden; trees, bushes, flowers and soil are represented.

Line — |design element| Materials that create a visual path for the eye to follow. Line forms the structural framework of a design.

M

Mille de Fleur — |style| "Thousands of flowers or blossoms" A design style made with many flower varieties and colors in a traditional fan-shaped or circular form.

Monochromatic Color Harmony — One pure hue plus tints, tones and shades of the same hue. |A hue + white = tint, hue + gray = tone, hue + black = shade|

N

Negative Space — |one type of space| Totally empty areas between flowers or materials.

New Convention — |style| A structured, linear-style design of vertical groupings reflected forward, backward and to the side at sharp right angles.

New Wave — |style| A design with materials altered |with paints, glue, etc| and placed in bizarre configurations resulting in conflicting lines.

O

Open Balance — |one type of balance| A term applied to a design's material placement when the characteristics of symmetrical or asymmetrical balance cannot be applied.

Open Form — A design shape which has spreading or radiating parts and space between the parts.

Oval |form| — An extension of a circular form, usually one-sided, in which materials flow in an extended circular pattern.

P

Parallelism — |technique| Two or more equidistant lines extending in the same direction. The lines never meet in, or radiate from, the same point.

Parallel Systems — |style| Two or more vertical groupings with negative space between.

Pavé — |style or technique| Design materials placed closely together in a cobblestone effect. |From jewelry design setting| Pavé can also be used as a technique in the base of a design.

Phoenix — |style| The regeneration of a round form with a tall burst of materials from its center.

Pillowing — |technique| Small clusters |or tufts| of flexible parts arranged closely together. The tufted groups flow like hills and valleys.

Positive Space — |one type of space| Area occupied by material.

Primary Colors — |red, blue and yellow| When mixed together in varying amounts they create all other colors.

Proportion — |design principle| The comparative size relationship between ingredients in a design.

Principles of Design — |composition, unity, proportion, accent, balance, harmony and rhythm| The primary ingredients in every floral design.

R

Rhythm — |design principle| The patterned repetition of a motif or formal element at regular or irregular intervals.

Right Triangle — |form| A type of asymmetrical triangle with the vertical line perpendicular to the horizontal line, forming a 90 degree angle.

S

Scale — |used in conjunction with the principle of proportion| The comparative size relationship of a design to its setting.

Scalene Triangle — |form| A type of asymmetrical triangle having unequal length sides and angles of different degrees.

Secondary Colors — |orange, green, violet| Created by mixing equal amounts of two adjacent primary colors.

Sequencing — |technique| Placing materials in the order of gradual or progressive change. Example: lighter to darker colors, or smaller to larger flowers.

Shadowing — |technique| A method of enhancing the visibility or impact of a material in a design by placing a second identical material behind and below the first.

Split-Complement Color Harmony — Created by mixing a hue on one side of the color wheel with the hues on either side of its direct complement.

Space — |design element| The three dimensional area in and around the design.

Static line — |one type of line| A line that follows the format of a design. Example: The vertical, perpendicular line within a rectangular format.

Symmetrical Balance — |one type of balance| Equal visual weight on both sides of a design's center axis.

Symmetrical Triangle — |form| A triangle having equal visual weight on both sides of its imaginary vertical axis.

T

Terracing — |technique| Materials placed in a series of levels rising one above another. The stair-stepping of materials.

Texture — |design element| The visible surface structure of a design's components.

Triadic Color Harmony — Three hues equally spaced on the color wheel. Example: The primary colors; blue, yellow and red.

True Form — A design that exactly follows the geometric principles of length, width and depth of a particular form.

U

Unity — |design principle| The relationship of individual parts to each other which produces a single general effect.

V

Value — |color theory| The relationship of a pure hue to the amount of white, black and gray mixed with it. Example: pink is a light value of red, burgundy is a dark value of red.

Vegetative — |style| To present materials as they grow in nature. Two types exist; radial and parallel. Radial vegetative means all design materials grow from one point. Parallel vegetative means equidistant groupings emerge from more than one point within the container.

Vertical — |form| A design which is taller than it is wide. The design's height is 1½ to 2 times the height of the container (or more). Design materials should not exceed the width of the container.

Void — |one type of space| Connecting space. Example: the clean stem of a flower connects it to the base of the design.

W

Waterfall — |style| Floral materials placed in a steep flow or extended cascade. Materials are placed in several layers that "spill" from a pool in the back of the design.

Western Line — |style| A lazy-L shape with the height 1½ times the width.

Z

Zoning — |technique| Restricting the numbers and types of materials used in specific larger areas.

Design
Principles

COMPOSITION

The seven PRINCIPLES OF FLORAL DESIGN (composition, unity, proportion, accent, balance, harmony and rhythm) are the constant, underlying ingredients in every floral design. Design elements (the interpretive ingredients) can be present, but they must be blended with these principles to create the overall composition.

All floral designs are first seen as a total composition. Each component within a design should contribute to its total look. In art terms, COMPOSITION is defined as the organization or grouping of different parts to achieve a unified whole. The word organization in the definition implies floral design is an exact thought process starting with the selection of the container, fresh materials and accessories and ending with their placement in the design.

Each of the materials in this composition contributes to the overall outcome of the design. First, the form of the design is evident: an asymmetrical triangle. The color of the materials and varieties of flowers are the next discovery. Also present is the repetition of shape beginning with the container and followed by the fuji chrysanthemum and daisy pompons, and ending with the spiral eucalyptus. All of these components— the form, color, varieties and repetition—are organized together to achieve the unified whole. If any parts of the composition are transposed or removed, design would be altered.

UNITY is a singleness of purpose. The relationship of the individual parts to each other should produce a single, general effect. The composition pictured below establishes a unified whole look because the materials are identical in color. The copper dried materials and container have a built-in unity because they have an identical metallic finish. However, not all designs need to have materials of the same color to achieve unity. Unity can be expressed in many other color harmonies and material selections, as long as they blend together to produce an intentional singular effect.

Sources: Light mauve saucer #725 from Rand Potteries, PO Box 237, Wynnewood, OK 73098.
Copper pottery container #12018T from Chimes, Inc, PO Box 444, Oswego, KS 67356. Copper sea grape, rye and eucalyptus from Knud Nielsen Company, available from your local wholesaler.

UNITY

UNITY

U nity can also be achieved by using different materials. The uncommon ingredients selected blend together to make a unified design. The flowers and foliages have different characters, colors and surface structures. Each component's placement is critical to achieving the impression of unity. Materials are grouped, with space between each collection, allowing the viewer to recognize and appreciate the different varieties.

Sources: Stoneware cylinder container #4008 in Sandstone, from Zanesville Stoneware Company, 309 Pershing Rd., Zanesville, OH 43701.

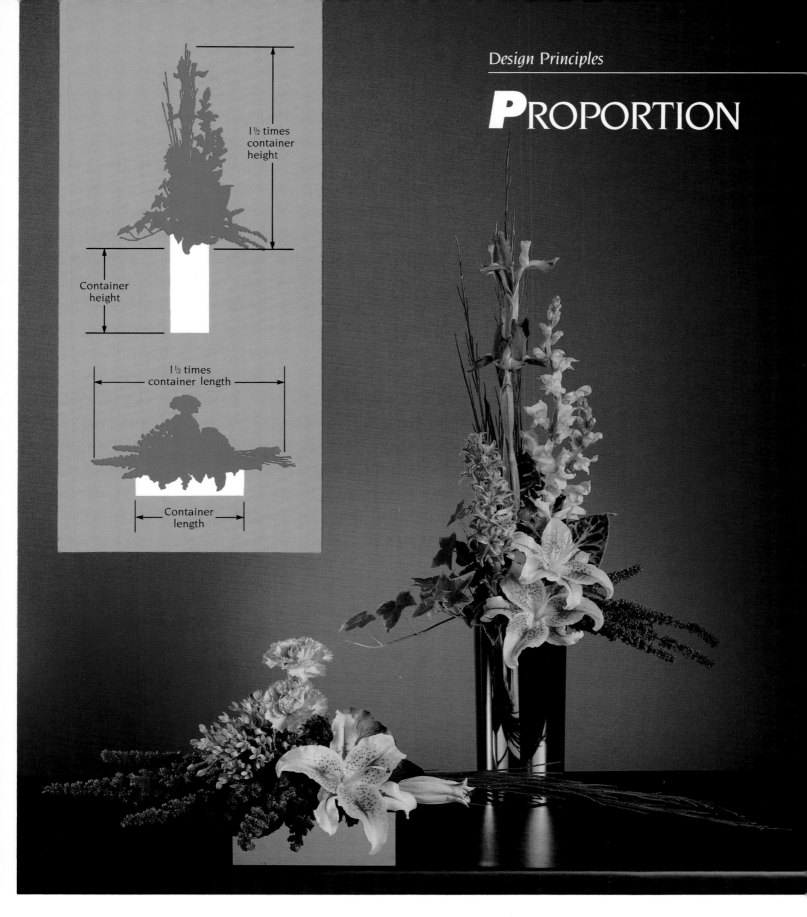

PROPORTION

PROPORTION is the comparative size relationship between ingredients within a design. This relationship can be measured in the quantity of flowers, length of stems or amount of materials used in a design. Setting the proportions for most floral designs begins with the container. The pair of compositions pictured are examples of standard rules of proportion. The taller vase fits the traditional 1½ to 2 times the height of the container rule. The horizontal design employs this same guideline using the container's length as a measurement.

The word SCALE is often used along with the principle of proportion. Scale specifically refers to the size of the arrangement in relation to its setting. For instance, a single flower bud vase would look out-of-scale on a 25-foot buffet table. However, several centerpieces used on that same 25-foot table would appear more in scale.

Sources: Chrome cylinder container from Producers Set II and chrome T-box from WSG Designs, 425 Huehl Rd. 6A, Northbrook, IL 60062.

ACCENT

Violets provide accent.

ACCENT in floral composition is a distinctive, regularly occurring, but subordinate pattern, motif or color. Traditionally, the focal area of a design is the place where accent is most recognized. The principle of accent is taken from music composition meaning "stress or emphasis given to certain notes."

The base of this vegetative composition is accented with pink African violet plants. The pattern of their placement attracts attention and establishes one of the focal areas of the design. Yet, the established pattern blends into the whole design picture. Within the application of accent in a design, the words, "regularly occurring" imply that each ingredient is repeated more than one time, as in the case of the violets.

Sources: Plastic saucer #P710 in Cactus Green from Franklin China, 816 Nina Way, Warminster, PA 18974.

BALANCE

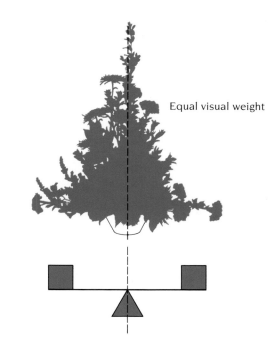

Equal visual weight

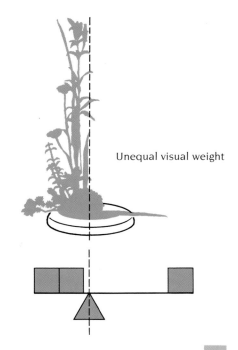

Unequal visual weight

The principle of BALANCE is achieved when the placement of the ingredients conveys a feeling of both physical and visual stability. PHYSICAL STABILITY refers to the actual placement of the main stems to establish the structure. If an arrangement is falling over because of poor stem placement, the physical balance or structure is faulty. VISUAL STABILITY is created by using color and material placement in sequence. An example of a visual stability rule is darker colors appear to be heavier and are used at the base of a design, lighter colors appear more lightweight and are used at the top of a design. Another example is the bud of a flower always appears lighter than a fully-opened flower of the same variety. So, buds are used at the top of a design, while fully-opened flowers are used at the base. Both physical and visual stability can be expressed in three ways: symmetrical balance, asymmetrical balance and open balance.

SYMMETRICAL BALANCE is characterized by EQUAL visual weight on each side of an imaginary vertical line. This equal visual weight does not have to be expressed in identical materials as pictured in the example of symmetrical balance. The center line reveals different materials on each side, yet the design appears to have equal visual weight on both sides and is symmetrically balanced.

ASYMMETRICAL BALANCE occurs when UNEQUAL visual weight appears on either side of an imaginary center line. The orange and peach composition is an example of asymmetrical balance. There is more visual weight to the left of the center line than on the right side.

OPEN BALANCE is a phrase used when neither symmetrical or asymmetrical characteristics can be applied to a design. Many of the newer design styles are classified as open balance. Abstract, new wave and parallel systems styles of design are all considered open balance because it is difficult to apply traditional balance fundamentals.

Sources: Similar beige pottery containers available from your local wholesaler.
Conch shell series 48 container from Lomey Mfg., available from your local wholesaler.

HARMONY

HARMONY is the pleasing aesthetic quality created by the careful selection of parts for a composition. It can be expressed in two ways: with similar, blending materials or contrasting components which are distinctively different. Harmony is most evident in design colors but can also be present in texture, shape, or size of materials.

This design is a mixture of garden variety flowers. Its harmony is expressed in the selection of materials that appear to have the same garden-grown look. Harmony is also expressed by the flowers' placement within the composition. All materials fit like the piece of a puzzle into the fan shape.

In contrast, two distinctively different flowers, for example tropical pink ginger and standard red carnations, can be combined in a harmonious design. These strongly different materials can be used together successfully if placed properly within a design. If the designer uses ginger as line material and carnations clustered at the base for texture, then the materials will appear to be in harmony.

RHYTHM

RHYTHM is the repetition of a motif or formal element at regular or irregular intervals. Rhythm can be expressed in line, form, color, spacing between flowers, or the simple repeating of curves or planes within a composition.

This yellow and peach composition illustrates rhythm with the repeated motif of the yellow lillies. The irregular placement of flower forms: two at the top, three in the middle and one at the base, shows an irregular repetition in the flow of the vertical line. Repetition used to express rhythm should not be dull. Using more than one form of flower (a spike flower and a round flower, for example) makes rhythm natural and visually stimulating.

Sources: Peach pink vase #8705 from Haeger Potteries, PO Box 558, Macomb, IL 61455.

Pattern of lillies expresses rhythm.

The five ELEMENTS OF FLORAL DESIGN (line, form, space, texture and color) are the interpretive components used by designers to create distinctive floral designs. For the greatest effect, these elements must be in harmony with the principles of design.

LINE creates the primary foundation of every design. It constitutes a visual path for the eye to follow. It also forms the structural framework of the design. There are two categories of line; static and dynamic.

A STATIC LINE is characterized by lack of unusual movement. A static line stays within the form of a design following its length, width, or depth.

A DYNAMIC LINE is active and is characterized by continuous movement. Within a square format, a dynamic line would exhibit a new direction (for instance, a curving line).

This design has both static and dynamic lines within the same composition. The lilies, tulips and iris create static lines that follow the rectangular form of the design creating a dynamic line. Dynamic lines energize everyday forms, adding zest and spirit to a design.

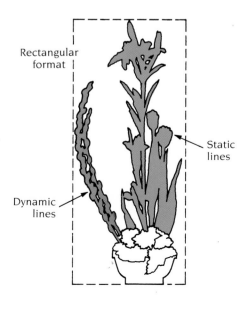

Rectangular format

Static lines

Dynamic lines

A static line as in the design above, exaggerated in length, becomes dynamic. The line of this composition exceeds the normal proportions of a horizontal design and is therefore classified as dynamic. This feeling or appearance is enhanced by the slight diagonal turn of the Featherwood™, adding to the visual interest of the composition.

Sources: Black bowl #624 from Lomey Mfg. Pickled pods from Knud Nielsen Company. Rainbow Cork from Advanced Floral Concepts, PO Box 693, Cedar Falls, IA 50613. Moss from HOH Grown, PO Box 2135, Forks, WA 98331.

Black container #505, Trendsetters Line from Syndicate Sales. Featherwood™ #576-04 from International Floral Fashions, Inc., 10119 W. Jefferson St., Culver City, CA 90232.

FORM

FORM is the external appearance of an area distinguished by the materials in a composition. Form is three dimensional; meaning length, width and depth. A TRUE-FORM design exactly follows the geometric principles of length, width and depth. There are closed forms and open forms, which are descriptive terms that apply to the physical characteristics of a design. A CLOSED FORM in floral design is a solid, compact or massed design. Biedermeier style designs are an example of a closed form. An OPEN FORM has spreading or radiating parts with space between the parts. A parallel-systems design is an example of an open form.

There are also classic and interpretive forms of design. These terms apply to the aesthetics of the design or its impression on the viewer. A CLASSIC FORM expresses simple harmony and could never be classified as "trendy" or a fad. It is timeless and will be considered "in style" for many years. An INTERPRETIVE FORM is simply a variation of a shape or a combination of shapes selected at the discretion of the designer. A full section of forms is found elsewhere in this edition.

A right triangle is a classic form because its characteristic dimensions are easily recognized. Orange gladioli create the 90 degree angle of the classic form. Marigolds and zinnias reinforce the angle as orange lilies fill in the remainder of the form. All the materials are exact in placement, making it a true-form example.

This bouquet of mixed garden flowers is an interpretive fan-shaped form. Primarily a radial form of design, this composition contains lines that break the classic form label. The extending lines of ivy interrupt the perfect outline of the fan shape. Also, some of the materials are placed in parallels, breaking the radial placement rule of fan-shaped form.

Sources: 6 inch Garden Pot #P1606 from Franklin China, 816 Nina Way, Warminster, PA 18974.
  Similar baskets available from your local wholesaler.

SPACE

SPACE is the three dimensional area in and around the design ingredients. The three types of space used in floral design are: positive space, negative space and voids.

POSITIVE SPACE is area within a composition occupied by material. A flower occupies a definite amount of positive space. Likewise, a massed, compact and solidly-filled design form occupies positive space. This symmetrical triangle of pompons occupies a definite, solid triangle form or positive space.

NEGATIVE SPACE is the empty area between flowers. As in music, it is the space between the notes that makes it more important. The empty space between the strong verticals in this parallel systems-composition is negative space. It adds important emphasis to the materials used.

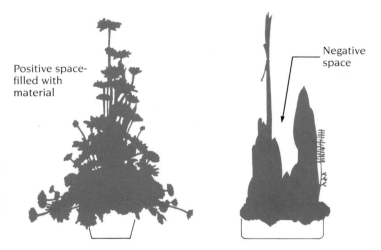

Positive space-filled with material

Negative space

Sources: Similar sandstone pottery containers are available from your local wholesaler.

Antique silver T-Box from WSG Designs, 425 Huehl Rd. 6A, Northbrook, IL 60062. Lt. green Rainbow Cork from Advanced Floral Concepts, PO Box 693, Cedar Falls, IA 56613. 18″ Forest green tapers from Creative Candles, PO Box 19514, Kansas City, MO 64141.

Space

VOIDS are connecting spaces. Often used in contemporary design styles, voids are clean and distinct lines that connect materials to the rest of the design. This composition is an example of a clearly defined connecting line (or void), in the clean stem of the fuji chrysanthemum. The stem connects the single blossom to the more elaborate base of the design. Voids allow the designer to use more dramatic space in a design.

Sources: Mauve pillow vase #661 from Rand Potteries, PO Box 237, Wynnewood, OK 73098. Chrome stripping available from your local hardware store.

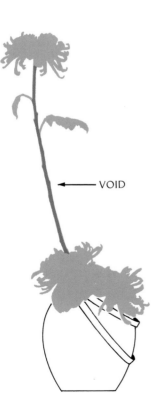

VOID

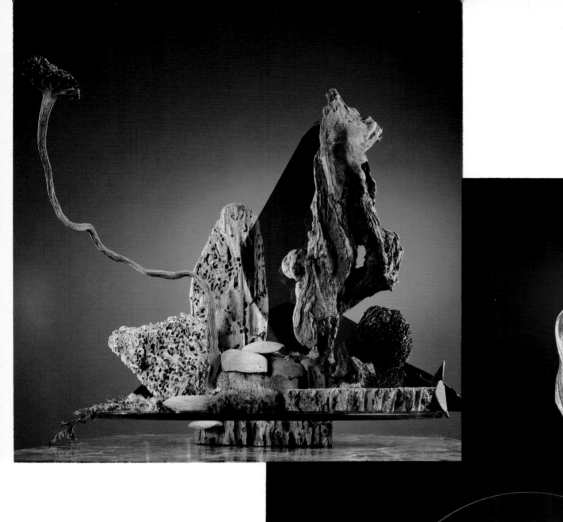

TEXTURE

TEXTURE is the visible surface structure of the materials used in a composition. Every material has specific characteristics that makes it unique. Leaves, blossoms, dried materials and other accessories used in a single design all contribute to the design's visual interest. Contrasting textures add a higher perception of quality to a floral design. Texture can be coarse or fine, smooth or rough, bright or dull.

The contrasting surface textures of wood, kelp, lichen and mosses sharply counter the smooth surface of the smoked glass shards used in the design. The composition is constructed on a clear glass disc adding to the texture contrast. Each individual ingredient is enhanced by the combination of the material textures.

Abstract designs often concentrate on texture and use the visual differences in the surface of materials for added impact. This composition contains a wide range of materials from fresh flowers to chrome, going to the extreme of using pieces of road paving. The high-tech feeling sets the stage for the presentation of a single white iris and a branch of Scotch pine. The two natural ingredients are more visually important because they contrast with the other materials.

Sources: Sahara II® dry flower foam from Smithers-Oasis. Rock moss #203, kelp strands #704, foliose lichen #434, spruce bark #421, teredowood slabs #705 and teredowood pieces #706, from HOH Grown, PO Box 2135, Forks, WA 98331.

Chrome containers, Producer's Set II from WSG Designs, 425 Huehl Rd. 6A, Northbrook, IL 60062. Silver sea grape leaves, strelitzia leaves and moss from Knud Nielsen Company.

COLOR

Color plays an important role in each arrangement. It can create a dramatic effect on the person who views it. All colors are beautiful; however, when colors are properly combined, the results are spectacular. Color gives a design personality by making a statement. Some colors are receding or relaxing in appearance, others are bright and cheerful or advancing.

HUE is the name of a full-intensity color. A color name could be simple, like red, or a compound name, like blue-violet.

CHROMA is the degree of intensity or purity of a hue. The term chroma is used to express the difference between a bright color and a duller shade of the same hue.

The VALUE of a color depends on the amount of white, black or gray that is mixed with a hue. Shades of a color are created by adding black to a hue. Tones are made by adding gray to a hue and tints are created when white is mixed with the pure hue.

The colors on the 12-hue color wheel used in teaching floral design can be classified into three distinct categories: primary, secondary and intermediate.

The PRIMARY COLORS (blue, red and yellow) when mixed together in varying amounts, create all other colors.

SECONDARY COLORS (orange, green and violet) are obtained by combining equal amounts of two adjacent (neighboring) primary colors. For example, secondary orange is created by mixing equal amounts of primary yellow and red.

INTERMEDIATE (or tertiary) COLORS are created by combining a primary color with a secondary color. For example, intermediate red-orange is created by mixing primary red and secondary orange.

Primary, secondary and intermediate hues are used in combinations called color harmonies.

MONOCHROMATIC

A MONOCHROMATIC COLOR HARMONY is achieved by using tints, tones and shades of the same hue. This monochromatic design begins with pink (a tint of red) and is presented in three differing values of pink from the deepest shade of the stargazer lilies to the palest pink of the snapdragons.

Sources: Light mauve saucer #725 from Rand Potteries, PO Box 235, Wynnewood, OK 73098.

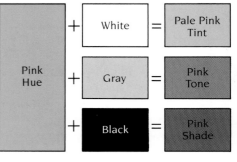

Pink Hue	+	White	=	Pale Pink Tint
	+	Gray	=	Pink Tone
	+	Black	=	Pink Shade

The Value Scale

ANALOGOUS

An ANALOGOUS COLOR HARMONY includes one primary color with adjacent (neighboring) colors on the color wheel. On a 12-hue color wheel, the analogous color harmonies fall within a 90 degree angle. This harmony cannot include more than one primary color. One of the three colors dominates the composition. An analogous color harmony can be extended by adding one or more colors on either side of the three chosen analogous colors. The red carnations, red-orange gerbera and red-violet dendrobium orchids are combined to create this analogous color harmony. To compose an extended analogous color harmony, the designer would add secondary orange and secondary violet.

Sources: Similar shape containers are available from WSG Designs, 425 Huehl Rd. 6A, Northbrook, IL 60062.

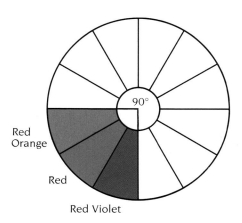

COLOR

COMPLEMENTARY

A COMPLEMENTARY COLOR HARMONY uses any two hues directly opposite each other on the color wheel. Blue and orange, green and red are examples of complementary color harmonies. The primary blue iris and secondary orange carnations and ranunculus of this composition create the dramatic effect achieved by using complementary colors.

Sources: Cobalt blue container #7005 from Zanesville Stoneware Company, 309 Pershing Rd., Zanesville, OH 43701. Moss from Knud Nielsen Company.

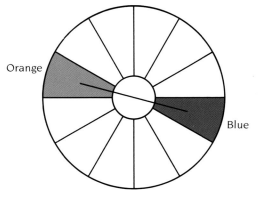

SPLIT COMPLEMENT

A SPLIT COMPLEMENT is created by mixing a hue on one side of the color wheel with the hues on either side of its direct complement. A composition of primary yellow gerbera combined with intermediate red-violet heather and blue-violet statice form this example of a split complementary color harmony.

Sources: Lavender mist pearlescent Series 49 container from Lomey Mfg., available from your local wholesaler.

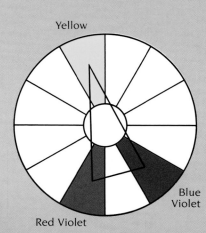

COLOR

TRIAD

A TRIADIC COLOR HARMONY blends three hues, equally spaced on the color wheel. The design pictured mixes the three primary colors; red carnations, yellow alstroemeria and blue iris to create a color triad. Any three hues (or tints, tones or shades of those hues) equidistant on the color wheel can be combined to create a triadic color harmony.

Sources: Cobalt blue container #4506 from Zanesville Stoneware Company, 309 Pershing Rd., Zanesville, OH 45701.

Design Forms

SYMMETRICAL TRIANGLE

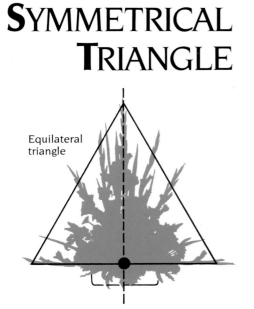

Equilateral triangle

SYMMETRICAL TRIANGLES occur when there is equal visual weight on both sides of the imaginary center axis. It is important to note, both sides of the center axis do not need to have identical material and placements. If the materials on both sides of the form are equal in visual weight, the triangular design is considered symmetrical. The purest appearance of this form requires an equilateral triangle, meaning all three sides are equal in length. Often symmetrical designs are isosceles triangles with the lengths of two vertical sides being equal.

This composition of all yellow flowers fills the definition of a symmetrical equilateral triangle. All sides of the triangle are equal in length, establishing the formal requirements of the style. If an imaginary line is placed through the center, the visual weight of the yellow flowers on both sides is equal.

Sources: Verde green rectangular CRB#2 container from Lomey Mfg., available from your local wholesaler.

ASYMMETRICAL TRIANGLE

A n ASYMMETRICAL TRIANGLE is a relaxed and visually impressive design. Its form is characterized by unequal visual weight on either side of an imaginary axis. There are two possible shapes for an asymmetrical triangle. One is a right triangle, with a sharp 90 degree angle and its tallest line perpendicular to the base. The other is a scalene triangle, with three unequal sides and angles.

This composition is an asymmetrical scalene triangle. The three main placements of gladioli meet at a traditional center focal point. The center of the design is filled with additional gladioli buds, foliage and roses which complete the asymmetrical scalene form. If an imaginary line is drawn through the center of the design, the right side of the triangle would have more visual weight.

Sources: Dusty Rose #15 French Rose Vase from Syndicate Sales. Green reindeer moss from Knud Nielsen Company. Both available from your local wholesaler.

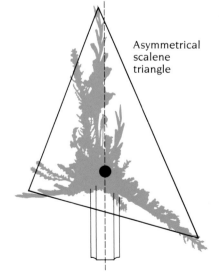

Asymmetrical scalene triangle

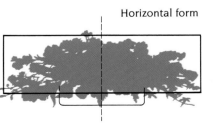

Horizontal form

HORIZONTAL FORMS are low, flat and tranquil designs. Their passive linear feeling is created by extending the length of the horizontal line for more impact. The standard length of a true horizontal form is 1½ to 2 times the length of the focal area. In its purest form the design has equal visual weight on both sides of the imaginary center axis.

Horizontal designs can be used as centerpieces when their passive line does not interrupt the evening's dinner conversation. This melange of pink, lavender and purple flowers is created by blending summer flowers with a horizontal form. The extended length of the design magnifies the impressive nature of its form. The design is balanced and has equal visual weight on both sides.

Sources: Lavender Mist CRB#2 container from Lomey Mfg., available from your local wholesaler.

27

VERTICAL

Standard rules of proportion (1½ to 2 times the height of the container) apply to a VERTICAL FORM composition. Some contemporary vertical designs extend this length to increase the form's dynamic impact on the viewer. A line drawn vertically from either side of the container should contain all flower placements in a true-form design version. The rule is materials should not exceed the width of the container. Many interpretations of this design form exist primarily due to the difficulty in restricting materials to the width of the diameter of the container.

Vertical form

A CIRCULAR FORM design has a sphere-like appearance. All the materials radiate from a single imaginary point (also called the binding point). This point is in the center of the container, below the edge. The circular form is usually compact and massed with flowers and has been interpreted by floral designers for centuries. In a true-form circular design, all the materials are placed within the circle. The overall appearance of the form should also have equal visual weight on both sides of the imaginary axis (which also bisects the imaginary binding point).

This interpretive circular form contains groupings of identical materials within the circle. The flowers have been organized this way to give an updated and contemporary look to this form. Two materials, the fern and curly willow, extend beyond the circle, and add interest and excitement to this traditional form. The exaggerated height of the container increases the contemporary feeling and is balanced by the mass of flowers at the top. This design is often placed in a lower container that seems to disappear when the composition is complete.

Sources: Light green tall cone vase #763 from Rand Potteries, PO Box 237, Wynnewood, OK 73098.

CIRCULAR

Sources: Azure blue candle holder/vase
from Blenko Glass Company,
Inc., PO Box 67, Milton, WV 25541.

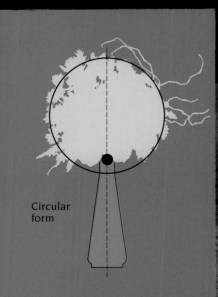

Circular
form

OVAL

Oval form

A n extension of the circular form, the OVAL FORM, follows many of the same principles. The circle shape is stretched into an oval and the materials continue to move in the extended circular pattern. The oval form is generally one-sided, and all the flowers are placed as if they flow in and out of one central imaginary binding point within the container.

The oval composition pictured contains strongly grouped materials. This technique gives the design a special personality and promotes the continuous oval swirling line as the eye moves from one group to the next. The entire shape is supported by the curving lines of Scotch broom at the base of the oval, which complement and accentuate the design form.

Sources: Brownstone container #5005 from Zanesville Stoneware Company, 309 Pershing Rd., Zanesville, OH 43701.

FAN-SHAPE

A FAN-SHAPE FORM is primarily a radial style or half circle. Linear flowers (snapdragons, gladioli, liatris, stock, etc.) are usually included in this design as they suggest the radiating lines of a sunburst or fan. Flowers with round forms fill in the areas between the radiating lines. The fan-shaped form is symmetrically balanced, giving the composition a formal and precise flair.

This example of a fan-shape form uses linear snapdragons, Scotch broom and eucalyptus to establish the radiating lines of the form. Pink carnations and foliage fill in between the lines, completing the design. Often used for funeral designs or church decorations, this form lends itself to masses of blossoms and makes an impressive floral display for the customer.

Sources: Amethyst Venetian bowl #427 from Island Images/Shorecraft, PO Box 802, Oak Harbor, WA 98277.

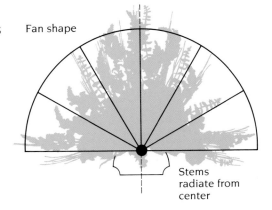

Fan shape

Stems radiate from center

CRESCENT

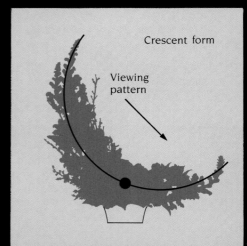

Crescent form

Viewing
pattern

A CRESCENT FORM is a portion of a circle (like the moon in its first quarter) created by an organization of floral materials. The motion of a smooth, curved line is essential to the design form. The lines of the form radiate from the container in a curved circular motion, forming a semicircle. The eye follows the continuous circular motion holding the viewer's attention and interest.

The curving lines of snapdragons establish the skeleton of this crescent form. Leptospermum, alstroemeria, roses and carnations fill in the three dimensional figure. This design is created with the highest portion of the semicircle to the left and the lowest portion to the right. This is a comfortable pattern when observing any work of art.

Sources: Seafoam green container #3606 from Zanesville Stoneware Company, 309 Pershing Rd., Zanesville, OH 43701.

The curved S-shape, commonly known as a HOGARTH CURVE, is adapted from the art world and is often interpreted in floral design. An English painter, named William Hogarth (1697-1764), first documented this "Line of Beauty" as the "basis for all successful artistic design." He wrote about this theory in his "Analogy of Beauty". The Hogarth curve has many variations ranging from S-shapes made of the same type of blossoms, to parts of the S-curve suggested by twigs, foliages or other materials. In its truest fashion, the S-shape is entirely made of the same materials. It has a formal and rigid appearance. Some of the early interpretations show definite patterns of materials in parallel rows forming the S-curves.

This all white example of a Hogarth curve relaxes the rigid S-curve by loosening the curves of the design. Stems are inserted into floral foam secured in a container. The container is attached to the top of the glass cylinder. The lazy-S shape is an interpretation of the traditional line of beauty created by Hogarth. Stock, bells of Ireland and dendrobium orchids form the curving S-shape. Roses, iris and ranunculus fill in the remainder of the figure.

HOGARTH CURVE

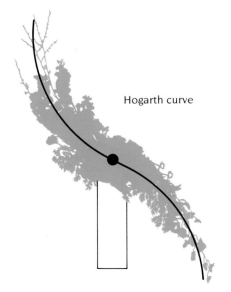

Hogarth curve

Design Techniques

BASING

Basing is a general term decribing techniques used to attractively detail a design's base. In the art world, the term basing applies to the physical stability given to a piece of sculpture at its base. In floral design, clustering and terracing are considered two basing techniques. They enhance the appearance of the design by adding color, texture and visual weight.

The foundation of this design is created by the contrasting textures and colors. Small clusters of kalanchoe blossoms and mood moss cover most of the base, while spiral cones and vertically placed salal leaves break the even patterns. The parallel placement of the composition's emerging materials further accentuates the basing techniques used.

Sources: Similar baskets are available from your local wholesaler. Pods on picks and Mini Designer Pod Collection from Knud Nielsen Company.

BASING
Materials fashioned in the design's foundation giving visual stability to the materials that emerge from it.

FOCAL AREA

A focal point is traditionally a single point where all materials meet or depart. That point is usually occupied by a single flower. Contemporary designers have expanded the single point definition and coined the phrase "focal area." A focal area is composed of more than one item and gains the attention of the person viewing it. It is larger than a focal point and often consists of contrasting textures and colors for added interest. Some contemporary designs contain more than one focal area.

This example of a focal area is composed of more than one type of material. All the materials converge in a larger area established by the lily buds. Contrasting textures of paper ribbon, foliage, pods and clear filler selected for the design enhance its appeal.

Sources: Black triangle container L-5 from Coronet Ceramics Corporation, 14520 Joanbridge, Baldwin Park, CA 91706. Black paper ribbon from Knud Nielsen Company. "California Crystals" from Ed Lenz Enterprises, Inc., 20 Bernice Dr., Freehold, NJ 07728.

FOCAL AREA
The area where all ingredients of a composition converge. The center of activity.

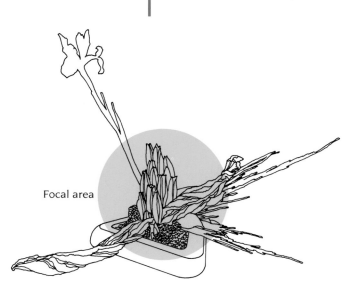

Focal area

35

Terracing is a basing technique. Identical materials, sometimes graduated in size, are placed in a horizontal, front to back, stair-step sequence. This technique can be applied to fresh flowers, foliages, dried materials or virtually any material used in a floral composition. Terracing adds texture and dimension to a design's base. Many natural materials grow in this stair-step pattern, making terracing a good technique for finishing the base of vegetative designs.

Several materials are terraced in this exquisite composition. Sea grape leaves, coculus leaves, small pieces of fungi and two gerbera are terraced in this example. The terracing technique employed here adds dramatic impact to the natural style design.

The repetition of the terracing technique in this design creates a sense of unity with a minimum amount of materials. The galax leaves, spruce bark and gerbera are carefully controlled in their placement and quantity. When a technique is repeated, one area of terracing should dominate. The terraced gerbera control the base and represent the greatest area of visual weight. The foliage and bark areas are smaller in appearance and are less dominant groupings.

Sources: Coral pink container #2710 from Zanesville Stoneware Company, 309 Pershing Rd., Zanesville, OH 43701. Reindeer moss, Spanish moss, Verdigris rye and sea grape leaves from Knud Nielsen Company. River root and fungi from HOH Grown, PO Box 2135, Forks, WA 98331.

Spruce bark from HOH Grown, PO Box 2135, Forks, WA 98331.

Leaves are terraced front to back.

TERRACING
Materials placed in a series of levels rising one above another; the stair-stepping of materials.

GROUPING

GROUPING
Identical materials (or colors) placed in a specific limited area with space between the individual parts.

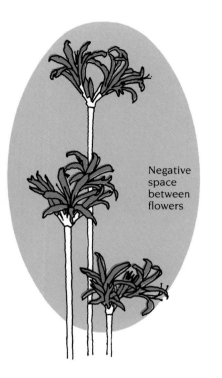

Negative space between flowers

Grouping is used to create an organized and planned feeling. Materials placed in groups have more impact than materials "polka-dotted" throughout a design. Grouping items allows the viewer to appreciate the individual variety, color, form or texture of the material and to properly distinguish it from others.

The materials in this composition are organized by variety and presented in groupings. Each defined area has ample space between the individual parts of the group, allowing the eye to discern the exact quantity, variety and color of the flowers. Even the foliages are grouped in confined areas, adding to the sense of order.

Sources: Gold container, Producer's Set II from WSG Designs, 425 Huehl Rd. 6A, Northbrook, IL 60062.

In floral design, clustering is a technique of placement. Items too small to be recognized as individual components are clustered for recognition as a single unit of color or texture. The technique of clustering could be used in the body of a design or to conceal part of the base.

This design uses clustering in two ways: to conceal part of the base and as part of the main body of the design. Several stems of nerine are clustered together and bound with gold bouillon. Red carnations, pink bouvardia and purple statice are clustered to conceal part of this contemporary design's base. Clustering these materials into solid color masses increases the visual impact of the composition.

Sources: Black pottery container #8314 from Sullivan, Inc., PO Box 1361, Sioux Falls, SD 57101.

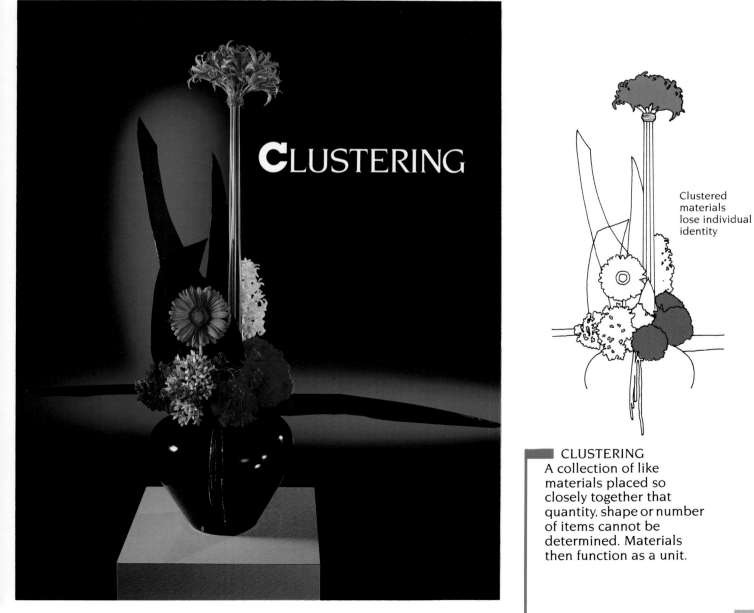

CLUSTERING

Clustered materials lose individual identity

CLUSTERING
A collection of like materials placed so closely together that quantity, shape or number of items cannot be determined. Materials then function as a unit.

ZONING
Restricting the numbers
and types of materials used
in specific larger areas.

ZONING

The term zoning applies to an area larger than a simple floral composition. Using the same principle of a zoned city or community, flowers can be zoned by variety or color into larger specific sections. An example of zoning is a 40-foot stage front decoration featuring a different color of flowers every five feet.

This contemporary mantel piece is a small version of the technique of zoning. Each dried material is specifically designated to a confined zone. The barn board base is finished with mood moss, spruce bark and stones uniting each vegetative zone.

Sources: Barn board base is painted with Celedon #764 Color Tool from Design Master. Sahara II® dry foam from Smithers-Oasis. Sage green bell cups, ting ting, lotus pods, sable palm and mood moss from Knud Nielsen Company. Spruce bark from HOH Grown, PO Box 2135, Forks, WA 98331.

SEQUENCING

Sequencing is the design technique which presents materials from smaller to larger sizes, from lighter to darker colors or from bud stage to fully opened blossoms. Sequencing materials is practical because many stems and bunches of flowers contain more than one size or stage of a variety. A general rule for sequencing flowers is to use light or small items on the outside of a design and the darker or visually heavier items toward the center or base. This simple rule helps to establish the design's visual balance.

Several materials in this composition are presented using the sequencing technique. The closed stargazer lilies begin at the top and progress to the largest, fully-opened blossom. The tulips and ranunculus buds follow the identical pattern of the lilies. The pattern these flowers follow is one set by nature: blooms at the bottom moving upward to the buds.

Sources: Mauve/burgundy container #751 from Rand Potteries, PO Box 237, Wynnewood, OK 73098.

SEQUENCING
Placing design materials
in order of gradual or
progressive change.

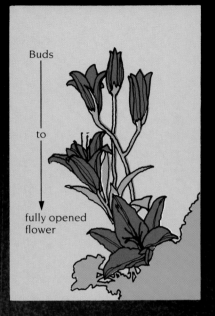

Buds

to

fully opened
flower

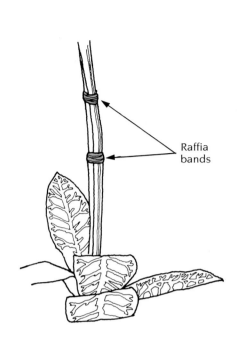

Raffia bands

BANDING

The technique of banding is used to accent or draw attention to a particular ingredient. In its purest form, banding serves no functional purpose, merely a decorative one. It is used as ornamentation, much like a person might wear a bracelet.

The bird of paradise stems in this example are banded with raffia as a decoration. The technique is repeated three times, drawing attention to the strong linear flower stems. The three raffia bands are contemporary accents and focus the eye of the viewer into a specific area within the composition.

Sources: Brown stoneware saucer #1008 S, from Zanesville Stoneware Company, 309 Pershing Rd., Zanesville, OH 43701. Raffia from Knud Nielsen Company.

BANDING
A thin, flat strip of a material surrounding a stem or container for decorative purposes.

Binding is the technique of physically fastening three or more stems together. The bunches formed by using this technique are restricted and supported by the substance binding them together. Binding is different from banding, because binding physically holds stems in place, as well as being attractive.

The binding of materials in the design pictured assimilates bunches of freshly picked flowers. The colored raffia holds the tulip, amaryllis and muscari stems in place restricting and giving physical support to this area of the design. The binding technique is a simple method of presenting materials with style and impact.

Sources: Blue floral ring #951 (half of the set of 2) from Island Images/Shorecraft, PO Box 802, Oak Harbor, WA 98277.

Raffia physically binds materials.

BINDING
The process of uniting
three or more like
materials by tying them
together in bunches.

BINDING

SHADOWING

Shadowing is a technique used to create the third dimension of depth. Single stems of materials (like foliage) can appear as flat surfaces. Placing an identical material in its shadow strengthens its visual weight and brings emphasis to the material.

Three foliages in this composition are used to illustrate the technique of shadowing. The galax, heliconia and dracena leaves each have more emphasis because of the second identical leaf placed directly behind them.

Sources: Similar pottery vases are available from your local wholesaler. Spanish moss from Knud Nielsen Company.

Second leaf shadows the first placement.

SHADOWING

A method of enhancing the visibility or impact of a material by using a second identical material behind and below the first placement.

Both flowers and foliages are shadowed in this composition of rich reds and oranges. The lilies, gerbera, roses and carnations are each shadowed by an identical flower. The fern fronds and dieffenbachia leaves are also shadowed by an identical frond or leaf. The technique is repeated six times, establishing a sense of unity.

Sources: Lichen from HOH Grown, PO Box 2135, Forks, WA 98331.

FRAMING

Framing is a technique of material placement that focuses the eye of the viewer on a specific area. Traditionally, materials are placed on the outside of a composition emphasizing a particular area (often the focal area). Occasionally, this technique can be used to isolate one specific ingredient. The technique takes its name from art masterpieces. Just as a beautiful frame calls attention to a gorgeous painting, the perimeter of a floral design can call attention to the flowers.

The stems of dried wild flowers frame the center kalanchoe blossoms in this dramatic example. The curving stems of the dried flowers lead the eye away from the design's center and return it again to enjoy the brilliant red-orange hue.

Sources: Bulb container #743 in Suntan from Rand Potteries, PO Box 237, Wynnewood, OK 73098.

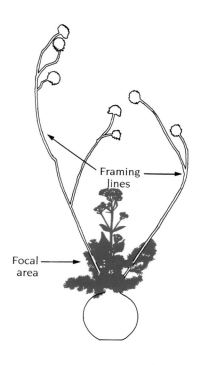

Framing
lines

Focal
area

▌ FRAMING

Materials placed in the perimeter of a design, fully or partially enclosing an area and focusing attention to the design's contents.

PARALLELISM

Parallelism is a method of placing materials in a floral composition. The equidistant lines may be horizontal, vertical or diagonal. In its purest form, parallelism appears stark and structural. It is a discipline of flower placement that requires long straight lines in groups of at least two.

The parallelism in this design is repeated in both flowers and foliages. Vertical parallel groups of identical materials are used at different heights within the composition. If the vertical lines of materials were extended indefinitely, they would not meet, but would be equidistant. Parallel lines can never radiate from the same point. They emerge from different points within the container.

Sources: Classic rectangular container CRB#2 in Lavender Mist, from Lomey Mfg. Black Rainbow Cork from Advanced Floral Concepts, PO Box 693, Cedar Falls, IA 50613.

Directions of Parallelism

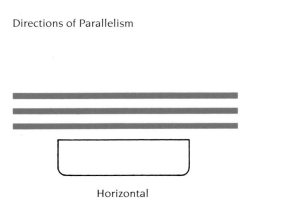

Horizontal

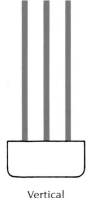

Vertical

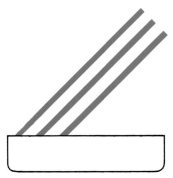

Diagonal

Traditional Design Styles

BIEDERMEIER

Traditional designs are timless. They resemble the styling or attitudes of an era and evoke nostalgic feelings. The "Biedermeier Style" of design was taken from a period in Germany and Austria between 1815–1848. This period is described as a time of conventionalism and romantic exuberance. Biedermeier styling is an adaptation of the French Empire era and shares similar characteristics. Compact circular and oval design forms and concentric circle material placements are part of the design's look.

The exact, concentric circles of this composition identify it as being from the Biedermeier period. Materials are restricted to specific rings or rows. Each row is composed of identically-sized components to keep the circular shape consistent. The contrast of the material's textures creates visual interest.

Another interpretation of Biedermeier styling occurs when the placements of concentric circles are loosened, as in this smaller example. The materials appear to be mixed throughout the composition, but they follow a planned pattern. The rows of materials blend into each other, softening the overall appearance of the design.

Sources: Utility Revere bowl from Syndicate Sales. Lettuce leaf container #PM903 from American Prestige, Inc., PO Box 19736, Little Rock, AR 72219.

MILLE DE FLEUR

Emerging from the same period of history as the Biedermeier is a style of design known as Mille de Fleur. The style name means "thousands of flowers or blossoms" and captures the romanticism of the time. Mille de Fleur designs are abundant in feeling and incorporate many colors and flower varieties. The classic-form design is fan-shaped to accommodate the vast quantity of flowers used.

This beautiful blend of flowers is classic Mille de Fleur styling. The symmetrical and patterned placement of materials and colors captures the essence of the style. The overabundant or opulent feeling is created by the large amount of material used in the design.

WATERFALL

Many believe "waterfall" is a new style of design, but the influence of this design can be traced back to the early 1900s. The waterfall look was first created for bridal bouquets in Europe at the turn of the century and is now enjoying a resurgence of interest as a container arrangement. The style is characterized by a steep flow of materials in an extended cascade. Flowing materials, such as bear grass, Asparagus sprengeri and plumosa are used to create the trickle effect. Reflective materials like bouillon, small shards of mirror and metallic thread are often used to capture the splashing light of a waterfall. Indicative of the style is the layering of ingredients to create depth. Yarn, feathers and other soft flowing materials can also be used in the design.

This waterfall design is accented with white standard roses. Waterfall compositions are so intricately detailed with small materials that some accent or emphasis is needed to make the design aesthetically pleasing. The floral foam is built up more than normal to accommodate the quantity of insertions and angle of the stems. The placement of the white roses is casual and without pattern, as if it had occurred naturally. All materials flow in the same direction from a "pool" of flowers at the back of the container.

Sources: Black Container #91−28 from Silvestri Corporation, 2720 N. Paulina St., Chicago, IL 60614.

INTERPRETIVE WATERFALL

This cascading interpretation of waterfall style is a bright and colorful classic design. The fresh materials flow in one direction from a "pool" of fruit and foliages. The dramatic curving line of bear grass accentuates the cascade of flowers. It repeats their placement as if it were a spray of water splashed from a rock below. The colors of the fruit and flowers are selected to blend and unite the centerpiece.

Sources: Brass candle stick and plate are a studio prop. Paper fruit from Hanford's, PO Box 32666, Charlotte, NC 28232.

PHOENIX

This style takes its name from the fabled bird that lives for 500 years or more, then destroys itself by fire and rises from its ashes to begin life anew. A phoenix design is the regeneration of a round form with a burst of materials from its center. The base arrangement is a traditional, compact radial design with very little space between the flowers. The style is fresh and eye-catching: the rebirth of a traditional form.

This phoenix design explodes with brilliant yellow forsythia from its center. A compact base of many flowers balances the tall extension of branches. Used as a delightful party centerpiece or home decoration, this distinctive look is impressive and is recognized as a timeless classic.

Sources: Forest green container #755 from Rand Potteries, PO Box 237, Wynnewood, OK 73098.

Natural Design Styles

A botanical-style design represents a study in the structure, properties and processes of plant life. It captures a plant's interaction with its physical environment. Each part of its life cycle is represented from the roots, to leaves, buds, flowers, and the end of life.

This botanical-style design portrays the essence of a tulip's life. The roots, and bulbs of the flowers have been exposed to tell the beginning of the story. A single tulip appears to be shattered by a passing breeze and its petals float gently to ground level. The design's base is covered in natural vegetation depicting the genuine environment where tulips thrive.

Sources: Brown spun saucer #1008 S, from Zanesville Stoneware Company, 309 Pershing Rd., Zanesville, OH 43701.

BOTANICAL

RADIAL VEGETATIVE

There are two types of vegetative-style designs. One is radial, the other parallel. Vegetative styling means presenting materials as they grow in nature. Vegetative designs are popular for they are a "scoop of nature" and evoke a feeling of tranquility and the simple life. In true form, vegetative designs follow a particular season: spring, summer, winter or fall. The seasons are not mixed. The earth line or soil is also represented by moss, rocks or low vegetation. There is usually more than one focal area, and the eye is encouraged to discover every facet of the design.

Radial-vegetative designs emerge from a single point. The white ranunculus are designed to appear as if they are growing. All materials radiate from a single imaginary point inside the container.

Sources: Blue pottery container #740 from Rand Potteries, PO Box 237, Wynnewood, OK 73098.

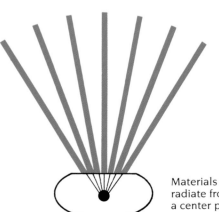

Materials radiate from a center point.

PARALLEL VEGETATIVE

This parallel-vegetative design interprets nature in spring. The materials are placed in vertical groupings equidistant at all points. The materials emerge from more than one point within the container, and are placed at varying heights. Moss and pods represent the earth or soil line and long strands of ivy soften the edge of the basket container.

Sources: Apple boat basket, smallest in set C516 from Nouvette Trading Ltd, Box 247, Oceanside, NJ 11572. Mood moss, mini designer pod collection from Knud Nielsen Company.

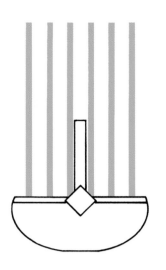

ZANDSCAPE

A landscape-style design presents a panoramic view of a garden area. It has a larger dimension than vegetative and includes trees, bushes, flowers and the ground level. The areas within the design are formal, organized and presented in color groupings. Plant material or patches of green are used as relief from brilliant bursts of color. Rocks, bark and other natural materials are placed as they are found in nature.

This example of a landscape-style design uses azalea branches to indicate the tree level of the garden. Three bells of Ireland stems resemble pine trees towering toward the sky. Heather and wax flower function as blooming shrubs and flowers emerge in definite, planned groupings. The ground level is patterned with mood moss, pods and lichen which cascade over the edge of the basket.

Fewer materials are used in this interpretive landscape style. Stripped branches of guava foliage represent the tree line, as the design quickly switches to the flower level of the garden. Tuberoses are clustered at the edge of the container and a single stem rises from the base. Two chrysanthemums take their own paths toward the sun and are supported by tiny bursts of eucalyptus. An avocado is nestled at the base as if it had just landed there. All these placements give viewers an impression they are seeing an untended garden or landscape. This example is an interpretative landscape style design.

Sources: Similar handled vine baskets are available from your local wholesaler. Lichen from HOH Grown. Natural gumbells from Schuster's of Texas, available from your local wholesaler.

Black oval container #505 from Syndicate Sales Trendsetters Line. Reindeer moss from Knud Nielsen Company.

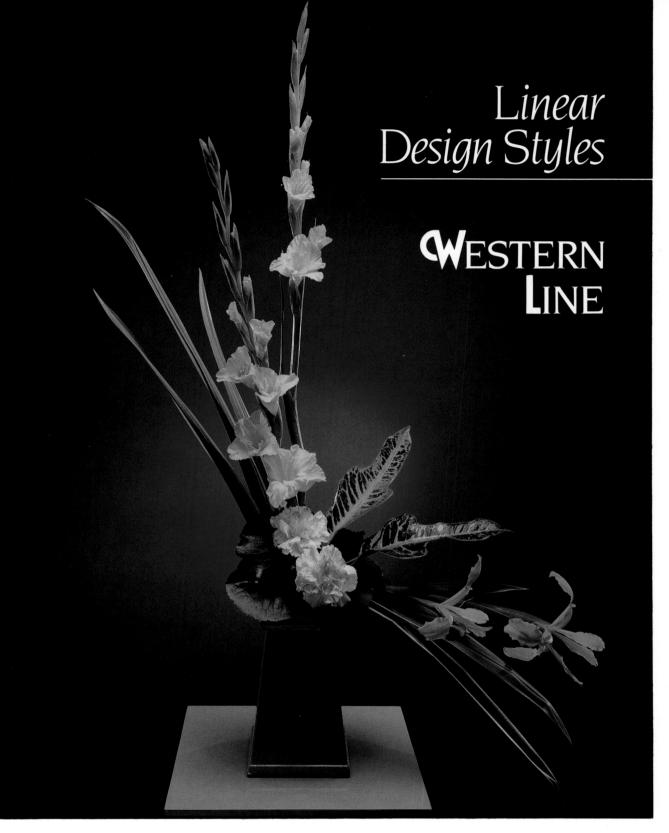

Linear Design Styles

WESTERN LINE

Western-line designs are known for their lazy or comfortable L-shape. In true form, the height of the design is 1½ to 2 times its width. This style is easily confused with an asymmetrical triangle. However, western line has a more flowing, comfortable L-shape. Some interpretations use the L-shape in a curving and sweeping line, in place of the established geometric line intersection.

Yellow gladioli, iris and carnations reinforce the comfortable L-shape created by the flax in this western-line style composition. The materials are grouped in pairs to add to the design's distinction. Two croton leaves contrast the expected flow of materials, and add visual interest to the style.

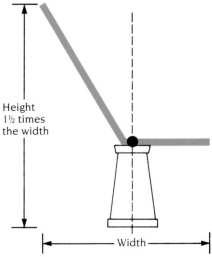

Height 1½ times the width

Width

ΦPARALLEL SYSTEMS

Parallel-systems style is composed of two or more vertical groupings with negative (empty) space between. This style uses the technique of parallelism to achieve its effect. In a true-form parallel system each vertical grouping should contain only one type of material. The composition's base should be clean and not interfere with the parallel vertical lines of materials.

This parallel system's example of liatris, celosia and snapdragons illustrates the principles of the style. The crisp movement of line is not diluted by any other materials. The floral foam is concealed by the flowers in the vertical grouping. In practical applications, the base of each grouping might be finished with foliage or moss. The parallels of material can be repeated several times if necessary, to increase the size of the design.

Sources: Dusty rose Design Tray #17 from Syndicate Sales, available from your local wholesaler.

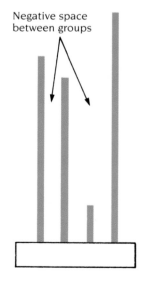

Negative space between groups

NEW CONVENTION

New convention is a structured, linear-style design. The vertical lines are reflected at sharp right angles, forward, backward and to the side. The reflected materials are identical to those in the vertical lines. Contrasting textures are used at the design's base where all the lines converge. A new convention design can have one or more vertical groupings. Each vertical line can be reflected. Negative (empty) space is used between vertical groupings for line definition.

This new convention-style design shows the forward, backward and side reflected lines of the vertical placements. The reflected lines are usually less dominant (shorter) than the vertical lines. The designer combines liatris and miniature carnations in each vertical line and distinctly separates reflected line materials by grouping them.

Some materials in the reflected lines of this new convention design are different from the materials in the vertical groupings. Strelitzia leaves and equisetum reflect the vertical lines of gladioli and tuberoses. The design's base is finished with the textures of moss and pickled lotus pods. The negative space between the two vertical groupings provides additional emphasis.

Sources: Black oval container #505 from Syndicate Sales Trendsetters Line.
Classic rectangular Verde Green CRB#2 container from Lomey Mfg. Pickled lotus pods and moss from Knud Nielsen Company.

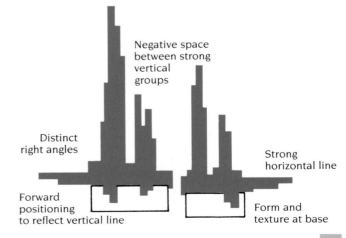

Negative space between strong vertical groups

Distinct right angles

Strong horizontal line

Forward positioning to reflect vertical line

Form and texture at base

ᚠORMAL LINEAR

A formal-linear composition has clearly defined lines and angles. The balance is always asymmetrical. The emphasis in a formal-linear design is on the shape and the form of the materials used, and how they fit into a composition. The lines can be vertical, horizontal or curving. Proportion (the size relationship of one part to another) is key to the successful execution of the style.

The opposite, curving lines of the equisetum and bear grass in this example establish the design's formal linear nature. Many forms and lines converge in the design's center: the shape of a pair of aspidistra leaves, the crescent shape of the single curved leaf, the two bowed lines of liatris, the slender line of curly willow and the intricate detail of the materials presented in clusters. The design's appearance is formal linear because of the emphasis on clean line, shape and form.

The straight lines created with strelitzia, bells of Ireland and the round form of curly willow designate the boundaries of this formal linear-style design. All materials in the composition are placed in groups adding to the design's distinction.

Sources: Similar containers are available from your local wholesaler. Moss from Knud Nielsen Company.
White oblong vase #701 from Rand Potteries, PO Box 237, Wynnewood, OK 73098.

Experimental Design Styles

PAVÉ

Pavé is a method of organizing materials as close together as possible with a cobblestone effect. The term is derived from jewelry design where identically-sized stones are set as close together as possible, to cover the base. Completely pavéd jewelry shows little or no metal between the stones and has nothing emerging from the surface. This example shows pavé as a style of design, however it can also be used as a technique in one part of a composition.

The design pictured shows pavé as a style of design. Materials are set close together, and nothing emerges from the surface. Each area within the limits of the container (or setting) is covered in identically-sized materials. Each section has a different color and texture adding to the distinction of the overall composition.

Sources: Red Rainbow Cork from Advanced Floral Concepts, PO Box 693, Cedar Falls, IA 50613. Mood moss, reindeer moss and Mini Designer Pod Collection from Knud Nielsen Company.

PILLOWING

Pillowing is a style achieved by placing materials in small clusters and flexible parts closely together. These "tufted" groups flow like hills and valleys on a landscape. Each little group "grows" from a separate point. There can be many points within a container where these tufted groups emerge.

Rich purple and pink flowers form this pillowing-style design. Some of the groups are larger or taller than others, creating the "hills and valleys" of the style. To add interest, the designer places extensions of heather, fern and curly willow which enlarge the visual space the design occupies.

Sources: Wild plum lily tray D-4 from A.L. Randall Company, PO Box 82, Prairie View, IL 60069.

New Wave

Sources: 6" red Designer Dish from Lomey Mfg. Basket handle from Syndicate Sales, sprayed with Holiday red #1438 and Lavender #1479 from Floralife, Inc. Yellow paper ribbon from Knud Nielsen Company.

Sapphire blue vase #872 from Blenko Glass Company. Stems sprayed with Aqua #702 Color Tool from Design Master. Panchu springs from Knud Nielsen Company.

New wave is a style which allows the designer's imagination to run wild. It became popular during the late 1970s and early 1980s when young people began altering their appearances with crazy colors, styles and materials. In floral design, new-wave styles are created by altering materials with paints, glue and other substances and placing them in bizarre configurations and conflicting lines. The accessories and containers are sometimes out of proportion with the rest of the composition. The balance of a new-wave design is considered open, as the guidelines of symmetrical or asymmetrical balance cannot be applied.

This new-wave design uses common materials in unexpected ways. Carnations are confined in position by the twisted, painted handle of a funeral basket. A piece of wire mesh supports a heliconia stem, which appears tied to the stem of a single peach gerbera. The base is a small red utility design dish finished with croton foliage and orange peelings. All the materials are placed for maximum visual impact and shock value fulfilling the new-wave style requirement.

A classically-shaped blue glass container is the start of this new-wave composition of altered materials. The tallest gerbera stem is topped by an inverted gerbera center which has lost its petals. Panchu springs swirl through the design with one stem bisecting the center of the lowest gerbera. The blue tubelike material is plastic plumbing from the hardware store. The stems of the gerbera have been painted aqua adding to the extreme nature of the design. Rolled sections of tubing have a section of gerbera glued into the folds. Each ingredient is altered or used in an unexpected manner in this design expression.

ABSTRACT

Abstract designs are freeform and emphasize color, shape and texture. They move away from the realistic presentation of materials and focus on unconventional and radical mechanical techniques. This freeform-abstract design presents some materials upside down, the opposite of how one expects to see them. Several lengths of heliconia stems are sliced at an angle and become design ingredients. All lines in this design are straight or static, with the exception of the curving gerbera stems and the heliconia flowers, which are dynamic. All materials are positioned in unexpected directions, yet, the composition is balanced and stable in appearance.

COMMON NAME SPELLING GUIDE
for Flowers, Foliages and Plants

Acacia [Mimosa]
African Violet
Agapanthus
Agave
Alchemilla
Allium
Alstroemeria
Amaranthus
Amaryllis
Anemone
Anthurium
Araucaria
   [Norfolk Island Pine]
Artichoke
Aspidistra
Aster
Astilbe
Azalea

Balsam
Bamboo
Banksia
Bayberry
Bear Grass
Begonia
Bells of Ireland [Moluccella]
Bird-of-paradise [Strelitzia]
Bouvardia
Boxwood
Brodiaea
Bromeliad
Browallia

Cactus
Caladium
Calathea
Calceolaria
Calendula
Calla
Camellia
Campanula
Candytuft
Carnation
Cattleya
Celosia
Chrysanthemum
Cineraria
Coleus
Cornflower
Crocus
Cyclamen
Cymbidium
Cyperus

Dahlia
Delphinium
Dendrobium
Dieffenbachia
Dogwood
Dracaena
Dusty Miller [Senecio cineraria]

Echeveria
Edelweiss
Eleagnus
Equisetum
Eremurus
Erica [Heather]
Eryngium
Eucalyptus
Euonymus
Euphorbia
Exacum [Persian Violet]

Fern
Ficus
Fiddleleaf
Firethorne
Flax
Forget-me-not
Forsythia
Freesia
Fuchsia
Fuji mum

Gaillardia
Galax
Gardenia
Ginger
Gladioli
Globe Amaranth
Gloxinia
Godetia
Goldenrod [Solidago]
Gorse
Grape Hyacinth [Muscari]
Guava
Gypsophilia

Heather [Erica]
Heliconia
Heliotrope
Hibiscus
Holly
Hollyhock
Honeysuckle
Horsetail
Hosta
Hoya
Huckleberry
Hyacinth
Hydrangea

Ilex Berries
Immortelle
Impatiens
Iris
Ivy
Ixia

Jasmine
Jerusalem Cherry
Jonquil

Kalanchoe

Kangaroo Paws
Kiwi Vine
Knife Blade Acacia
Kochia

Larkspur
Laurel
Lavender
Leptospermum
Leucadendron
Liatris
Ligustrum
Lilac
Lily
Lily-of-the Valley
Lisianthus
Lotus
Luneria [Silver dollars]
Lycopodium

Magnolia
Mahonia
Maidenhair
Manzanita
Marigold
Mimosa [Acacia]
Ming Fern
Mistletoe
Mitsumata
Moluccella [Bells of Ireland]
Monkshood
Monstera
Montbretia
Monte Casino
Muscari [Grape hyacinth]
Myrtle

Nandina
Narcissus
Nasturtium
Nephthytis
Nerine
Nigella
Norfolk Island Pine
   [Araucaria]

Oleander
Oncidium
Orchid
Oregonia
Ornithogalum

Palmetto
Pampas Grass
Pansy
Paphiopedilum
Papyrus
Peony
Peperomia
Periwinkle
Phalaenopsis
Philodendron

Phlox
Pittosporum
Plumosa
Podocarpus
Poinsettia
Poppy
Primrose
Primula
Protea
Prunus

Ranunculus
Rhododendron
Rose
Rudbeckia
Ruscus

Safflower
Salal
Salvia
Sanseveria
Saponaria
Scabiosa
Scotch Broom
Shasta Daisy
Smilax
Snapdragon
Solidago [Goldenrod]
Solidaster
Spathiphyllum (Peace lily)
Sprengeri
Staghorn Fern
Statice
Stephanotis
Stock
Strawflower
Strelitzia [Bird-of-Paradise]
Streptocarpus
Sweet William

Thistle
Thyme
Ti leaves
Torch Ginger
Trachelium
Tritoma
Tuberose
Tulip

Verbena
Veronica
Viburnum
Violet

Waratah
Waterlily
Waxflower
Wisteria

Yarrow
Yucca

Zinnia

THE PROPER CARE AND HANDLING
of Fresh Flowers

The quality of your shop's fresh flowers depends on your commitment to their care and handling. Follow these steps to improve customer satisfaction.

PREPARING YOUR SHOP

SCRUB UP!
Clean everything that comes into contact with fresh flowers by using a warm detergent-bleach solution. This will prevent the spread of bacteria. At least weekly |daily is better| clean tools, refrigerators, knives and counter tops. Clean buckets used for flower storage after every use; commercial bucket cleaners are available.

KEEP TRASH CANS COVERED
Stems and foliage in trash cans |and on floors| should be removed often. These deteriorating materials create ethylene gas which damages flowers. Keep all cans of discarded stems and foliage covered to reduce the amount of ethylene damage.

CHOOSE THE RIGHT CONTAINER
Use plastic or glass containers. Metal containers corrode easily and corrosion can contaminate the water and shorten the life of flowers.

CHECK THE TEMPERATURE AND HUMIDITY
Check the temperature and humidity of your refrigerators constantly. At least every six months have the unit checked by a professional. Most flowers need 34° F and a minimum humidity level of 80% to 90% is ideal. Some flowers |like orchids and tropicals| require warmer temperatures. See section on care and handling of specific flowers.

USE HIGH QUALITY WATER
Poor water quality with excessive contaminates block the movement of water up the stem. Have your shop's water tested by a commercial water purification company. The water in your shop should have less than 200 parts per million total dissolved solids. It is best to use distilled, reverse osmosis or deionized water.

PROCESSING YOUR FLOWERS

UNPACK IMMEDIATELY
Internal heat builds up in closed boxes and can damage flowers. Open box lids if you cannot properly process flowers immediately.

INSPECT ALL SHIPMENTS
Report any quality problems to your supplier immediately.

REMOVE FOLIAGE FROM STEMS BELOW WATER LINE

Foliage in water creates bacteria and causes flowers to deteriorate. Remember to remove damaged flowers and leaves, because they can carry bacteria and produce ethylene gas which destroy flowers.

CUT STEMS UNDER WATER

Flowers cut under water have a distinct advantage; water speeds up the stem to rehydrate the flower. When flowers are not cut under water, air gets into the stem and blocks the flow of water, causing the flowers to wilt.

Underwater cutting machines speed up the cutting process—especially for medium to large size shops. Flower stems can also be hand-cut under water. Place the stems in a warm water preservative solution. Make sure water is retained on the stem ends during this transfer.

USE PRESERVATIVES

The correct amount of the right preservative will enhance the quality, color and lasting ability of your flowers. Always follow the instructions for measuring and mixing preservatives. Measure the water capacity of the buckets and containers you use to store flowers to help determine the proper amount of preservative.

AIR CIRCULATION IS ESSENTIAL DURING PROCESSING

Always loosen bunches and sleeves to allow the flowers to open normally. This will also help condition them properly.

NEVER LEAVE FLOWERS OUT OF WATER

When designing, select flowers from the cooler and place them in a bucket containing warm water and a preservative solution. Take the bucket to your design table to prepare the arrangement. Flowers out of water for long periods should be re-cut under water before being used.

EDUCATE YOUR CUSTOMERS

Each arrangement leaving your shop gives you the opportunity to educate the customer. Attach a care and handling card that gives instructions on when to add water, proper temperature and any other special care instructions. Simple care and handling tags with your shop's name can be designed and printed by a local company. Commercial care tags are available through your local wholesaler.

Tell customers to re-cut all loose cut flowers under water in their kitchen sink. A quick demonstration of this technique is also helpful. Give customers a sample packet of preservative with their purchases.

SPECIAL CONDITIONING FOR IMPROVING VASE LIFE

CITRIC ACID

This short-term pre-treatment is for water-stressed crops such as roses and gerbera. This process balances the water for the pre-treatment solution to 3.0-3.5 ph level. This step is important because it enhances water absorption and increases vase life.

TO USE—Follow the manufacturer's instructions on the label of the citric acid granules. Cut flowers under water and place them in the citric acid solution at least 10 to 12 inches deep for one hour. Then transfer the flowers to a clean glass or plastic container with a properly mixed preservative solution.

STS—[Silver Thiosulfate]

Conditioning with STS greatly improves the vase life of ethylene sensitive crops such as carnations, alstroemeria, miniature carnations, cornflower, delphinium, gladioli, lilies, freesia, snapdragons and stock. This treatment prevents the rolling and browning of petals and aids in flower opening. It also prevents floret abscission and prolongs the vase life of some crops up to 150%. STS treatment is most effective when it occurs just after the crop is harvested. Before using an STS treatment in your shop check with your grower to see if the specific crop has already been treated. More than one treatment can harm flowers.

ENVIRONMENTAL NOTE: It is illegal to dump most brands of STS solutions down your drainage system. To dispose of STS solutions, use a silver exchange column system. These are available from the same companies that manufacture STS. Read the label carefully, some brands of STS are disposable.

TO USE—Follow the mixing instructions on the label. Place flowers into the STS solution for the amount of time specified on the label. [Usually, not longer than one hour.] Transfer flowers to a warm preservative solution after they have been conditioned for the appropriate amount of time in STS. Follow the label instructions for disposal. Re-cut stems after conditioning and transfer to water treated with a preservative.

TIPS ON THE CARE AND HANDLING of Flowers

ALSTROEMERIA

General care:
- Unpack immediately to prevent wilting.
- Cut stems underwater.
- Remove foliage below water line.
- Remove damaged flowers and yellow foliage.
- Refrigerate at 34° F, 80-90% humidity.

To improve vase life:
- Use STS [Silver Thiosulfate] for one hour if the crop has not been pre-treated.
- Let flowers soak up water for 1 to 2 hours before refrigerating.
- Use a floral preservative of your choice.

ANTHURIUM

General care:
- Unpack immediately.
- Cut stems underwater.
- Do not refrigerate [below 50° F].
- Keep humidity level at 80-90%.

To improve vase life:
- Place flower heads in deep water for one hour.
- Trim stems and place in a warm preservative solution, using the solution of your choice.

BOUVARDIA

General care:
- Remove as much foliage as possible.
- Cut stems underwater.
- Refrigerate at 34° F.
- Keep humidity level at 80-90%.

To improve vase life:
- Use STS for one hour if the crop has not been pre-treated.
- Use the floral preservative of your choice.

BIRD-OF-PARADISE & HELICONIA

General care:
- Unpack and remove protective paper coverings.
- Cut stems underwater.
- Do not refrigerate [below 50° F].
- Keep humidity level at 80-90%.

To improve vase life:
- Use the floral preservative of your choice.
- Loosen florets in sheath so flowers will open.

CARNATIONS

General care:
- Unpack and remove foliage below water line.
- Cut flowers underwater.
- Condition overnight at room temperature [especially for dry-packed carnations].
- Refrigerate at 34° F.
- Keep humidity level at 80-90%.

To improve vase life:
- Use STS for one hour if flowers were not pre-treated.
- Store flowers in a warm preservative solution.

CHRYSANTHEMUM

General care:
- Unpack and strip foliage below water line.
- Discard damaged flowers and foliage.
- Cut stems underwater.
- Let flowers absorb water before refrigeration.
- Refrigerate at 34° F.
- Keep humidity level at 80-90%.

To improve vase life:
- Use the floral preservative of your choice.
- Be careful not to dislodge petals, or the entire flower could shatter.

DAFFODIL

General care:
- Condition flowers separately. Do not mix with other varieties. Daffodils secrete a substance during conditioning which is harmful to other flowers.
- Condition for 3 to 6 hours at room temperature.
- Refrigerate at 34° F.

To improve vase life:
- Use special bulb flower preservative.

FREESIA

General care:
- Unpack and cut stems underwater.
- Condition at room temperature for 2 to 4 hours.
- Refrigerate at 34° F.
- Keep humidity level at 90%.

To improve vase life:
- Use STS for one hour if crop has not been pre-treated.
- Use a bulb flower preservative.

GERBERA

General care:
- Suspend flowers with heads supported by original packing or chicken wire. Place 4 to 6 inches of the stems in water with a preservative solution.
- Stems should not touch bottom of container during conditioning.
- Condition at room temperature for one hour.
- Refrigerate at 34° F.
- Keep humidity level at 80-90%.

To improve vase life:
- Use water without fluoride.
- Keep containers clean.

IRIS

General care:
- Unpack and cut stems underwater.
- Remove foliage below water line.
- Loosen bunches to allow flowers to open.
- Refrigerate at 34° F.
- Keep humidity level at 90-95%.

To improve vase life:
- Condition every 1 to 2 days by re-cutting the stems.
- Replenish the supply of preservative in the water.

LILIES

General care:
- Unpack and give each stem ample room to open.
- Remove the anther from the stamen (pollen stains clothing).
- Store above 40° F or at room temperature.

To improve vase life:
- Use STS treatment for one hour at the most, if flowers were not pre-treated.
- Use the floral preservative of your choice.

ORCHIDS

General care:
- Remove flowers from vials and re-cut stems.
- Refill the vials before placing the re-cut stems.
- Store at temperature above 50° F.

To improve vase life:
- Keep water off flower surface, it may cause spotting.
- Slice only a small portion of the stem each time you re-cut it. The stems are very short.

PROTEA

General care:
- Cut the stems, do not smash them.
- Remove foliage below the water line.
- Store at room temperature.

To improve vase life:
- Use the floral preservative of your choice.
- Hydrating pre-treatments are helpful.

TULIPS

General care:
- Unpack and cut stems underwater.
- Keep flowers in sleeves they help support weakened stems.
- During conditioning place flowers in 4 to 6 inches of warm (100° F) water with a preservative.

To improve vase life:
- Use a bulb flower preservative.
- Store at 34° F, 80-90% humidity.
- Stems continue to grow or elongate after harvesting. When using tulips in arrangements, plan for their growth.

THE CARE AND HANDLING OF ROSES

Each year millions of roses are sold across North America. The popularity of this flower has made it America's National Flower. Retail florists are concerned about the proper care and handling of this highly perishable crop. Here are some easy-to-follow suggestions to improve the vase life of your flowers.

Inspection — Open each box of roses immediately. Check for quality and quantity ordered. Report any problems to supplier immediately.

Stripping — Foliage below the water line must be stripped. Foliage in water breeds bacteria which can harm flowers. Removing foliage can be done three ways: mechanically with a special motorized machine, manually with a hand-held foliage stripper or by hand while wearing heavy gloves. Do not damage the stem of the rose. If the outside tissue is injured, you may damage the tubes that carry water to the flower.

Sanitation — Bacteria clogs stems and causes roses to die prematurely. Always clean buckets after every use. Tools, and counter tops should be disinfected regularly. Keep refrigerator free of all non-saleable, broken or inferior products, as they produce ethylene gas. This invisible gas shortens a flower's life. Keep fruits, vegetables and lunches out of the refrigerator.

Education — Every employee in your shop needs to be trained to use proper care and handling techniques. It is especially important that your employees pass on proper care and handling methods to the customer. Every package of roses (and other flowers, too) should have care instructions on a printed card.

Hydrating Solutions — A citric acid treatment can be used to hydrate roses. If your roses are not taking up water correctly, this treatment can eliminate early wilting, bent neck or poor development. Prepare the citric acid solution following directions on the package. (There are commercially available buffered treatments from your local wholesaler.) After the roses have been properly cleaned and cut underwater, place the stems in 10 to 12 inches of the solution for one hour at room temperature. Then, transfer the roses to warm water with a floral preservative added. *Always mix preservative according to the manufacturers instructions.* Don't guess!

Follow these six steps for maximum rose vase life.

1. SANITATION — clean containers, buckets and surfaces with a substance designed to kill bacteria.

2. REMOVE FOLIAGE — Any foliage below the water line must be removed.

3. CUT STEMS UNDER WATER — This keeps air in the stem to a minimum and speeds water to the head of the flower.

4. USE A FLORAL PRESERVATIVE — Test different products with the water in your area. Mix preservative in warm water, approximately 100° to 110° F.

5. REFRIGERATE AT 34° to 36° F — High humidity (90%) is also recommended. Keep refrigerator free of ethylene producing agents.

6. EDUCATE YOUR CUSTOMER — A small card with instructions and a sample package of preservative is helpful in educating your customers.

INDEX

Abstract, *page* 64
Accent, *page* 10
Analogous, *page* 21
Asymmetrical Triangle, *page* 26
Asymmetrical Balance, *page* 11
Balance, *page* 11
Banding, *page* 42
Basing, *page* 34
Biedermeier, *page* 48
Binding, *page* 43
Botanical, *page* 53
Chroma, *page* 20
Circular, *page* 29
Classic Form, *page* 16
Closed Form, *page* 16
Clustering, *page* 39
Color, *pages* 20-24
Common Name Spelling Guide,
    page 65
Complementary, *page* 22
Composition, *page* 6
Crescent, *page* 32
Design Elements, *pages* 14-24
Design Forms, *pages* 25-33
Design Principles, *pages* 6-13
Design Techniques, *pages* 34-47
Dynamic Line, *page* 15
Experimental Design Styles,
    pages 61-64
Fan Shape, *page* 31
Focal Area, *page* 35
Focal Point, *page* 35
Form, *page* 16
Formal Linear, *page* 60
Framing, *page* 46
Grouping, *page* 38
Harmony, *page* 12
Hogarth Curve, *page* 33
Horizontal, *page* 27
Hue, *page* 20
Intermediate Colors, *page* 20
Interpretive Waterfall, *page* 51
Interpretive Form, *page* 16
Landscape, *page* 56
Line, *page* 15
Linear Design Styles, *pages* 57-60
Mille de Fleur, *page* 49
Monochromatic, *page* 20

Natural Design Styles, *pages* 53-56
Negative Space, *page* 17
New Convention, *page* 59
New Wave, *page* 63
Open Balance, *page* 11
Open Form, *page* 16
Oval, *page* 30
Parallel Systems, *page* 58
Parellel Vegetative, *page* 55
Parallelism, *page* 47
Pavé, *page* 61
Phoenix, *page* 52
Physical Stability, *page* 11
Pillowing, *page* 62
Positive Space, *page* 17
Primary Colors, *page* 20
Proportion, *page* 9
Quick Reference Glossary, *pages* 4, 5
Radial Vegetative, *page* 54
Rhythm, *page* 13
Scale, *page* 9
Secondary Colors, *page* 20
Sequencing, *pages* 40, 41
Shade, *page* 20
Shadowing, *pages* 44, 45
Space, *pages* 17, 18
Split Complement, *page* 23
Static Line, *page* 15
Symmetrical Triangle, *page* 25
Symmetrical Balance, *page* 11
Terracing, *pages* 36, 37
Texture, *page* 19
The Care and Handling of Fresh
    Flowers, *pages* 66, 67
Tint, *page* 20
Tips on Care and Handling,
    pages 68, 69
Tone, *page* 20
Traditional Design Styles, *pages* 48-52
Triad, *page* 24
Unity, *pages* 7-8
Value, *page* 20
Vertical, *page* 28
Visual Stability, *page* 11
Void, *page* 18
Waterfall, *page* 50
Western Line, *page* 57
Zoning, *page* 40

ILLUSTRATIONS

Accent, *page* 10
Analogous Color Harmony, *page* 21
Asymmetrical Triangle, *page* 27, *top*
Asymmetrical Balance, *page* 11, *bottom*
Banding, *page* 42, *top*
Binding, *page* 42, *bottom*
Circular, *page* 29
Clustering, *page* 39, *bottom*
Complementary Color Harmony,
    page 22
Crescent, *page* 32
Directions of Parallelism, *page* 47
Fan Shape, *page* 31
Focal Area, *page* 35
Framing, *page* 46
Grouping, *page* 39, *top*
Hogarth Curve, *page* 33
Horizontal, *page* 27, *bottom*
Negative Space, *page* 17, *right*
New Convention, *page* 59
Oval, *page* 30
Parallel Systems, *page* 58
Parallel Vegetative, *page* 55
Positive Space, *page* 17, *left*
Proportion, *page* 9
Radial Vegetative, *page* 54
Rhythm, *page* 13
Sequencing, *page* 41
Shadowing, *page* 44
Split Complement Color Harmony,
    page 23
Static/dynamic Line, *page* 15
Symmetrical Triangle, *page* 25
Symmetrical Balance, *page* 11, *top*
Terracing, *page* 37
Triadic Color Harmony, *page* 24
Value Scale, *page* 20
Vertical, *page* 28
Void, *page* 18
Western Line, *page* 57